Key to Advanced

KEY TO
ADVANCED LATIN

Stephen Anderson,
James Morwood
and Katharine Radice

Bristol Classical Press

First published in 2009 by
Gerald Duckworth & Co. Ltd.
90-93 Cowcross Street, London EC1M 6BF
Tel: 020 7490 7300
Fax: 020 7490 0080
info@duckworth-publishers.co.uk
www.ducknet.co.uk

A catalogue record for this book is available
from the British Library

ISBN 978 1 85399 730 3

Typeset by Ray Davies
Printed and bound in Great Britain by
CPI Antony Rowe, Chippenham and Eastbourne

Contents

1. Translations of Unseen Translation/Comprehension Exercises

1. Mistaken tactics

There was a veteran in Caesar's army, Gaius Crastinus, who had served with him in the previous year as first centurion in the tenth legion, a man of outstanding courage. When the signal was given, he said, 'Follow me, you who have been my comrades, and give your general the service you have resolved upon. This one battle remains; when it is over he will regain his honour and we our freedom.' At the same time, looking at Caesar, he said, 'I shall today give you reason, my general, to thank me whether I am alive or dead.' When he had said this, he was the first to run forward from the right wing, and about 120 picked men of the same cohort serving as volunteers followed him.

Between the two lines there was only sufficient space left for the two armies to charge against each other. But Pompey had previously instructed his men to await Caesar's attack and not to move from their position, and to allow his line to be broken up; he was said to have done this on the advice of Gaius Triarius so that the intensity of the soldiers' first charge should be broken and their line stretched out, and so that his own men, drawn up in their ranks, should attack a scattered enemy; he hoped that the spears would fall with less serious effect on his men if they were held back in their position than if they themselves threw their missiles and advanced. But this action of Pompey's seems to us to have been done with no reason, especially since there is in everybody by nature a certain innate keenness and enthusiasm of spirit which is fired by dedication to the fight; generals should not stifle this but foster it; and there was good reason for the custom in the old days that signals should blare forth from every side and all should raise a shout; they reckoned that by these means the enemy were terrified and their own men urged on.

Caesar, *De Bello Civili* 3.91-2

2. Terrified flight

But when Pompey saw his cavalry driven back and noticed that the part of his army in which he had the greatest confidence was utterly terrified, feeling no trust in the rest either, he left the battlefield and immediately rode to his camp, and to those centurions whom he had set in position at the praetorian gate he said loudly, so that the soldiers could hear him, 'Protect the camp and defend it carefully if anything worse happens. I am going round the other gates and encouraging the guards of the camp.' After he had said this, he went to the general's tent with no confidence in his fortunes but still waiting to see what would happen.

When Pompey's men were driven in flight inside the rampart, Caesar, thinking that no respite ought be to given to the utterly terrified enemy, encouraged his men to exploit the kindness of fortune and to attack the camp. Although they were exhausted by the considerable heat (for the action had lasted until midday), even so their spirit was ready for every labour and they obeyed his command. The camp was being stoutly defended by the cohorts which had been left there to guard it, and much more keenly still by the Thracians and the barbarian auxiliaries. For the soldiers who had fled from the battlefield were both terrified in spirit and shattered with exhaustion; very many of them had thrown away their arms and their military standards and were thinking more about continuing to flee than about the defence of the camp. And indeed those who had taken up position on the rampart could no longer withstand the large number of missiles, but shattered with their wounds, they left their position, and immediately all of them, using the centurions and the tribunes of the soldiers as their guides, fled to the very high hills which stretched up to the camp.

Caesar, De Bello Civili 3.94-5

3. Pompey is killed

There by chance was King Ptolemy, a boy in years, who was waging war with considerable forces against his sister Cleopatra, whom a few months before with the help of his relations and friends he had driven from the throne; and the camp of Cleopatra was not far away from his camp. Pompey sent to him requesting that he might be received in Alexandria in view of the hospitality and friendship he had shown his father, and that he might be protected in his calamity by Ptolemy's resources. But those who had been sent by him, after they had completed the obligations of their embassy, began to speak more freely with the king's soldiers and to encourage them to show their sense of duty to Pompey and not to despise his fortunes. In this number were several soldiers of Pompey whom Gabinius had taken from his army in Syria and had transported to Alexandria and, after the completion of the war, had left with Ptolemy, the boy's father.

Then, when they found out about this, the friends of the king, who were in charge of the kingdom on account of his youth – whether induced by fear, as they afterwards declared, or in contempt of his fortunes, as generally speaking friends become enemies when disaster strikes – replied generously in public to those who had been sent by him and told him to come to the king; but they themselves engaged in a secret scheme and sent Achillas, the prefect of the king, a man of remarkable boldness, and Lucius Septimius, to kill Pompey. He himself, after being addressed with magnanimity and led on by some acquaintanceship with Septimius embarked on a tiny little ship with a few of his men; thereupon he was killed by Achillas and Septimius.

Caesar, *De Bello Civili* 3.103-4

4. Plans to leave

When they thought that they were ready for this plan, they set fire to all their towns, about twelve in number, their villages – about four hundred – and the remaining private buildings. All their grain, except what they were likely to take with them, they burnt, so that once hope of returning home had been taken away they might be more ready to meet every danger. They persuaded the Rauraci, the Tulingi and the Latobrigi, their neighbours, to burn their towns and villages and to set out at the same time with them; the Boii, who had lived across the Rhine and had crossed into Noric land and attacked Noreia, they joined to themselves as allies.

There were in total two routes by which they could leave home: one was through the territory of the Sequani, narrow and difficult in between the Jura range and the river Rhone, so that even in single file carts could scarcely be taken there; a very high mountain towered over it with the result that only a few men could block their way easily. The other was through our province, and was much easier because the river Rhone flows in between the territory of the Helvetii and the Allobroges and there is a crossing in several places in shallow water. The last town of the Allobroges and the nearest to the territory of the Helvetii is Geneva. From that town a bridge stretches across to the Helvetii. They thought that either they would persuade the Allobroges, because they seemed not yet to be well disposed towards the Roman people, or they would forcibly compel them to let them go through their territory. When everything had been made ready for their departure, they named the day on which all were to meet at the banks of the Rhone.

When it had been announced to Caesar that they were trying to travel through our territory, he hastened his departure from Rome and arrived at Geneva.

Caesar, De Bello Gallico 1.5-7

5. Druids

But out of these two groups, one is made up of Druids, the other of horsemen. The latter take part in holy rituals, look after sacrifices public and private, and interpret religious matters: a large number of adolescents go to them for the sake of training and the Druids are greatly respected by them. This is because they make decisions about almost all disputes, public and private, and, if any crime has been committed, if there has been a murder, if there is a dispute about inheritance or lands, again, they judge and they decide the rewards and the penalties. If anyone – either an individual or a race – does not abide by their decision, they are banned from the sacrifices. This punishment is the most serious among them. Those for whom it is thus forbidden are counted among the number of the impious and the wicked, and everyone deserts them and flees away from their approach or conversation, for fear that they might by contagion suffer some harm. Justice is not given when they ask, nor is any status shared with them. Over all these Druids, one is in charge; this man has the greatest standing among them. When he dies, if there is someone from the remainder who has a pre-eminent position, he takes his place; if there are several who are comparable, then by a vote of the Druids and sometimes even by armed combat they contest the leadership. At a fixed time of the year, in the territory of the Carnutes (this region is thought to be in the middle of all Gaul), they meet in a sacred place. To this place from all directions come all those who have disputes, and they obey their decisions and judgements. Their doctrine is thought to have been discovered in Britain and brought from there into Gaul and now, those who wish to understand the matter more carefully, for the most part set out there in order to learn.

Caesar, *De Bello Gallico* 6.13

6. A mysterious oracle

A terrible portent appeared to Tarquinius as he was doing this: a snake slithered out from a wooden column, and when it had caused fright and flight in the palace, didn't so much strike the heart of the king himself with sudden terror as fill it with anxious forebodings. Therefore, although only Etruscan soothsayers were used for public prodigies, terrified by this apparently domestic sight he decided to send to Delphi, the most famous oracle in the world. And not daring to entrust the oracle's replies to anyone else, he sent two of his sons over lands at that time unknown, and seas more unknown, to Greece. Titus and Arruns set out; and with them as a companion went Lucius Junius Brutus, son of the king's sister, Tarquinia, a young man actually of very great ability, but who had put on a pretence of stupidity in order not to be put to death by his uncle. He was then taken to Delphi by the Tarquinii, to be honest, more as a butt of their humour than as a companion.

When they had arrived there and carried out their father's instructions, a desire entered the young men's hearts to enquire to which of them the kingship of Rome was going to come. From the depths of the cave, they say, was returned the utterance: 'The first of you, young men, to give a kiss to his mother will have supreme power at Rome.' The Tarquins gave orders that the matter should be kept strictly secret, and themselves decided by lot which of the two of them should be first to kiss their mother when they had returned to Rome. But Brutus, thinking that the Pythia's words meant something else, as if he had slipped and fallen, touched the earth with a kiss, on the grounds that she was the common mother of all mortals.

Livy 1.56

7. A clever thief

He first fortified the Palatine Hill on which he had been brought up. He performed sacred rites to the other gods and to the Greek Hercules, as they had been established by Evander. They say that after Hercules had killed Geryon, he drove off his wonderfully beautiful cattle to this region, and close to the river Tiber, just where he had swum across driving the herd in front of him, in a grassy area where he could refresh the cattle with rest and abundant food, he too lay down in his exhaustion after his journey. Heavy with food and wine, he fell into a deep sleep there. Then a shepherd called Cacus who lived near that place, a man who was fierce because of his great strength, was attracted by the beauty of the cattle and wanted to steal them as his plunder. But because if he drove the herd into his cave by leading them, their very tracks would lead their owner there in his search, he turned around some cattle, all of them of outstanding beauty, and dragged them into his cave by their tails. When Hercules woke at daybreak, he looked over his herd and realised that some of its number were missing and went to the closest cave to see if there were footprints leading to it. When he saw that they were all pointing outwards and yet weren't leading anywhere else, in his confusion and uncertainty he began to drive his herd away from the dangerous place. As the cattle were being driven off, some of them lowed, as often happens, because they missed those who had been left behind. An answering low from those shut up in the cave made Hercules turn back. When he was coming towards the cave and Cacus tried to stop him by force, Hercules hit him with his club and he died, calling in vain upon the shepherds to help him.

Livy 1.7

8. A disastrous love affair

Not only did a blush pour over Masinissa when he heard this, but tears too welled up; and when he had said that he would indeed be subject to the general's control, and had begged him to have regard– as far as the matter allowed – for his word, rashly given (for he had promised that he would not hand her over into anyone's power), he withdrew from the headquarters to his own tent. There, when he had spent some time in frequent sighing and groaning, which could easily be heard by those standing around the tent, giving a huge groan he called a trustworthy man from among his slaves and ordered that he carry poison mixed in a wine-cup to Sophonisba, and at the same time announce that Masinissa was keeping his word, that she should not end up while alive in the power of the Romans: mindful of her father the commander, her homeland and the two kings to whom she had been married before, she should act in her own best interests.

When the slave, carrying this message and the poison at the same time, had reached Sophonisba, she said, 'I accept the wedding gift, nor is it unwelcome, if my husband has been able to offer nothing better to his wife: however, tell him this, that I would have died better, if it had not been at my funeral that I married.' The ferocity of her words was no greater than the courage with which she took the cup and drained it, giving no sign of fear. When this was announced to Scipio, so that the hot-headed young man might not plan something more serious, he summonded him straight away and now consoled him, now gently reprimanded him, because he had paid for his rashness with more rashness, and had made the matter more tragic than it had to be. On the next day, so that he might turn his mind away from its current commotion, he climbed up upon the dais and ordered that a meeting be called. There, having first called him king and bestowed upon him exceptional praise, he gave to Masinissa a golden crown, a golden bowl, the curule chair and ivory sceptre, and an embroidered toga and a tunic decorated with palm branches.

Livy 30.1

9. Extreme patriotism

Thus from there the armies were led back home. Horatius went in first place, bearing his three-fold battle spoils before him. His maiden sister, who had been betrothed to one of the Curiatii, met him in front of the Porta Capena. When she recognised on top of her brother's shoulders her fiancé's cloak which she herself had made, she untied her hair and weeping called her dead fiancé by name. His sister's lamentation in the midst of his own victory and such great public joy stirred the heart within the hot-tempered young man. And so drawing his sword and at the same time rebuking her out loud he stabbed the girl. 'Go from here with your ill-timed love to your fiancé,' he said, 'forgetful of your brothers dead and alive, forgetful of your country. So perish any Roman woman who mourns an enemy.' That crime seemed dreadful to the senators and to the people: but his recent service counted against the deed.

During his trial, the people were influenced especially when his father Publius Horatius proclaimed that he judged that his daughter had been rightly killed: if it were not so, he would have punished his son with a father's entitlement. Then he begged them not to make him, whom just a little before they had seen with outstanding progeny, bereft of his children. During this, the old man, embracing the young man and pointing out the spoils of the Curiatii, said, 'Are you able, citizens, to see this man, whom just now you saw in procession, honoured and rejoicing in victory, bound under the furca amidst beatings and torture? Go, lictor, tie up his hands, which in arms just recently won power for the Roman people. Go, cover up the head of the liberator of this city; hang him from a barren tree.' The people could bear neither the tears of a father, nor Horatius' own spirit, constant in every danger, and they acquitted him, more from admiration of his courage than the justice of his case.

Livy 1.26

17

10. Hannibal schemes again

Hannibal, in exile from his homeland, had arrived with Antiochus and was held in high esteem by the king, on no other recommendation than that for him, long turning over in his mind plans for a war against Rome, no-one could be a more appropriate participator in conversation on such a matter. His opinion was always one and the same, that war should be waged in Italy: Italy would supply both provisions and troops for a foreign enemy; but if there were no movement there and the Roman people were allowed to wage war outside Italy with Italian strength and forces, neither the king nor any race would be a match for the Romans. He demanded for himself a hundred ships, ten thousand infantry and a thousand cavalry; with that fleet he would first make for Africa; he had every confidence that the Carthaginians could be induced by him to rebel; if they delayed, he would stir up a war against the Romans in some part of Italy.

When he had brought the king round to this view, he thought that that he ought to prepare the minds of the Carthaginians for this, but didn't dare to write a letter, in case by some mischance it might be intercepted and lay open his plans. He had picked up at Ephesus a certain Tyrian called Aristo, and after trying out his skill on less important tasks, he loaded him partly with gifts and partly with the hope of rewards, and sent him to Carthage with his instructions. He gave him the names of those whom he needed to meet, and equipped him with secret signs, by which they would recognise without doubt the instructions as his. When this Aristo appeared in public at Carthage, Hannibal's enemies discovered for what reason he had come just as soon as his friends. At first the matter was a conversation topic at dinner parties. Then some began to say in the senate that nothing had been achieved by Hannibal's exile if in his absence also he could disturb public security.

Livy 34.60-61

11. An unusual friendship

'In the Circus Maximus,' he said, 'a fight consisting in a hunt on a huge scale was being presented to the people. Since I happened to be at Rome,' he said, 'I was a spectator at this event. There were many savage wild animals there, the vast size of the beasts was notable, and either the appearance or the fierceness of all of them was unusual. But beyond everything else, the huge size of the lions awakened admiration, and one of them beyond all the rest. This one lion had caused the minds and the eyes of everyone to focus on him by the momentum of his body, his vast size, and his terrifying and resonant roaring as his muscles rippled and the hair of his mane streamed. The slave of a man of consular rank who had been allocated to fight with the wild beasts had been brought on among several others; this slave was called Androclus. When that lion saw him at a distance, suddenly,' he said, 'he stood still as if in wonder and then went up to the man gradually and calmly as if recognising him. Then he wagged his tail in a friendly and gentle manner exactly in the same way that fawning dogs do, made contact with the man's body and gently licked the legs and hands of the slave, who was now almost dead with fear. Amid these affectionate actions of such a fierce wild beast, the man Androclus regained his lost wits and gradually turned his eyes to look at the lion. Then, as if they had recognised each other,' he said, 'you could have seen the man and the lion joyously congratulating each other.' He said that this so utterly amazing event aroused very loud shouting from the people and that Androclus was summoned by Caesar and the reason was sought as to why the very fierce lion had spared him alone. Then Androclus told an amazing and wondrous story.

Gellius 5.14

12. Biological warfare

In a few days' time they were going to fight a decisive naval battle. Hannibal was inferior in the number of ships: he had to fight by trickery since he was not equal in arms. He ordered as many poisonous snakes as possible to be gathered alive and put into earthenware jars. When he had got together a large number of these, on the very day on which he was about to fight the naval battle, he called together his marines and instructed them all to concentrate their attack on King Eumenes' ship alone, and to be satisfied with merely defending themselves against the rest. This they would easily achieve because of the large number of snakes. Moreover, he would see to it that they knew in which ship the king was sailing; if they either captured or killed him, he promised that it would earn them a great reward.

After he had encouraged his soldiers in this way, the fleets were brought out for battle on both sides. When their line had been put into position, before the signal for battle could be given, Hannibal made it clear to his men where Eumenes was. The king did not hesitate to join battle at once. When they clashed together, the Bithynians, at Hannibal's instruction, attacked Eumenes' ship all together. Since the king was not able to withstand their might, he sought safety in flight, which he would not have secured had had he not retreated inside his own defences which were located on the nearby shore. When the remaining Pergamene ships began to assail their opponents more keenly, the earthenware vessels, about which we made mention above, suddenly began to be hurled upon them. On being thrown, these initially stirred up laughter among the combatants, and there was no understanding as to why this was happening. However, after they saw their ships filled with snakes, they were terrified by the strange turn of events, turned their ships round and retreated to their naval camp.

Nepos, *Life of Hannibal* 10.4-11

13. Grief at leaving home

When there comes to my mind the very sad picture of that night which was my final time in the city, when I revisit the night on which I left so many things that are dear to me, even now too a teardrop slips from my eyes. The dawn was nearly here, the day on which Caesar had ordered me to depart from the furthest boundaries of Italy. There had been neither time nor spirit for getting ready the sort of things which were needed: our hearts (*or* my heart) had become numb over the long wait. I took no thought over choosing slaves or a companion, no thought for clothing or help suitable for an exile. I was dumbfounded just like a man who is struck by Jupiter's thunderbolt and lives on and is unconscious of his own existence. However, when my very sorrow took this cloud from my mind and at last my senses grew strong, I spoke for the last time to my sad friends as I was about to go away: of the many there had recently been there were just one or two. In her love my wife held me as I wept, weeping more bitterly herself as a shower of tears continually fell down her cheeks which did not deserve it.

Ovid, *Tristia* 1.3.1-18

21

14. Pious disobedience

And now they were lying, heavy with both food and wine, and with sleep, and there was deep repose throughout a carefree Argos: around me I seemed to hear the groans of dying men, and in fact I had heard them, and what I feared was true. My blood departed, heat left both mind and body, and, cold now, I lay on my newly-wedded couch. Just as slender ears of corn are set quivering by the gentle Zephyr, or as a cold breeze shakes poplar leaves, either thus, or even more, did I tremble. You yourself lay still, and the wine I had given you was the wine of slumber. My violent father's commands struck away my fear; I raised myself and with trembling hand took the weapon. I shall not speak falsely. Three times my hand raised the sharp sword, three times, having wickedly raised the blade, it fell again. I moved it to your throat – let me confess to you the truth – I moved my father's weapon to your throat; but fear and piety blocked the cruel deeds of daring and my pure right hand shunned the task laid upon it.

Ovid, *Heroides* 14.33-50

15. Deification

There is a place – the ancients called it the Marsh of Caprea. There by chance, Romulus, you were giving judgements to your people. The sun fled, clouds, moving beneath it, obscured the sky, and a heavy shower fell with torrents of water. Here it thundered, there the sky was riven with streaks of lightning. The people fled, and the king made for the stars on his father's horses. There was mourning, the senators were falsely charged with murder, and that belief might perhaps have stuck in men's minds; but Julius Proculus was coming from Alba Longa, the moon was shining and there was no need of a torch, when the hedgerow on his left quivered with a sudden movement; he stepped back, and his hair stood on end. Handsome, larger than in life and adorned in a robe, Romulus seemed to be present in the middle of the road, and at the same time to have said: 'Stop the citizens mourning, and let them not violate my divinity with their tears; let them offer incense, and let them, a pious throng, appease the new Quirinus and cultivate their ancestral skills and the art of war.' He gave his orders, and vanished from sight into thin air. Proculus called the peoples together and reported his words as bidden.

Ovid, *Fasti* 2.491-510

16. Different ambitions

We started our education right away while we were still young, and thanks to our father's care for us we went to the men of the city who were famous because of their skill. My brother aimed at public speaking from his youngest years: he was born for the warfare of the wordy law court. But as for me the holy rites of poetry were what gave me pleasure even in my boyhood and the Muse stealthily drew me into her work. Often my father said, 'Why do you engage in a useless pursuit? Homer himself left no wealth behind him.' I was moved by his words, and, totally abandoning Helicon, I tried to write words freed from metre. Of its own accord my song fell into the appropriate metre, and what I tried to write was verse. Meanwhile, as the years went by with silent tread, the toga which gave more freedom was taken up by my brother and by me and the broad purple stripe was put on my shoulders, and our enthusiasms remained as previously they were. And now my brother had reached the age of twenty when he died and I began to miss a part of myself.

Ovid, *Tristia* 4.10.15-32

17. A terrible storm

And the terrible south wind casts away my words and does not allow my prayers to go to the gods to whom they are addressed. And so the same winds – so that I should not be harmed only in one respect – carry our sails and prayers I know not where. Wretched me! What huge mountains of water are surging! You would think that any moment now they will touch the highest constellations. What huge valleys sink down as the sea is parted! You would think that any moment now they will touch black Tartarus. Wherever I look there is nothing but sea and air, the former swollen with waves, the latter threatening with clouds. Between the two of them the winds roar with an immense roar. The wave of the sea does not know which master to obey. For now the east wind takes its strength from the purple East, now Zephyrus is here sent from the West (lit. the late evening). Now the freezing north wind rages from the dry North, now the south wind wages its battles from the oppose direction. The helmsman is at a loss and cannot find what to flee or to make for: his very skill is nonplussed by the conflicting evils.

Ovid, *Tristia* 1.2.15-32

18. An unwelcome lover

He looks at her hair hanging unadorned from her neck and says, 'What if it were adorned!' He sees her eyes flashing with fire just like stars, he sees her lips, which it is not enough merely to have seen; he praises her fingers and her hands and her forearms and her upper arms, more than half bare; the parts of her that are hidden he thinks even better. She flees more swiftly than the light breeze and does not stop at these words as he calls her back: 'Nymph, daughter of Peneus, stay, I beg you! I do not pursue you as an enemy; nymph, stay! Thus the lamb flees the wolf, the deer the lion, thus doves flee from the eagle with fluttering wing: all of them are fleeing their enemies: love is my reason for pursuing you! Wretched me! I fear that you may fall down flat and brambles may mark your legs which do not deserve to be hurt and I may be the cause of your pain. The areas through which you are rushing are rough: run at a more moderate pace, I beg you, and slow down your flight, and I shall follow at a more moderate pace myself. However, ask who it is that you are pleasing to. I am no inhabitant of the mountain, no shepherd, I am no uncouth guardian of the herds and flocks here. You do not know, you rash girl, you do not know whom you are fleeing, and that is why you are fleeing.'

Ovid, *Metamorphoses* 1.497-515

19. Hopeless love

'I am that boy: I understand, nor does my reflection deceive me. I burn with love of myself: I both ignite the flames and feel them burn. What am I to do? Am I to be asked or do the asking? What then shall I ask? The thing I desire is right here with me: my abundance has made me poor. O that I were able to leave my own body! Would that – a strange wish for a lover – the thing I love were far away. Now pain takes away my strength, and no long space of my life remains, and I am destroyed completely at the very beginning of my life. Death is not burdensome for me, since in death I shall lay aside my sufferings. I wish that this boy, who is cherished, could be longer-lived. As it is, we – two hearts that beat as one – shall die in a single breath.' He spoke and returned, scarcely sane, to the same reflection and rippled the waters with his tears. As the pool moved, the image came back to him obscured. When he saw this disappearing, he shouted, 'Where are you fleeing to? Stay here and don't – cruel one – abandon me, your lover! Let me be allowed to look at what cannot be touched, and to offer sustenance for my wretched passion!' While he grieved, he pulled his tunic down from the neckline, and he beat his bare breast with his marble-white hands.

Ovid, *Metamorphoses* 3.463-481

20. Savage revenge

She had spoken, and from the taut bow the bow-string sounded, which terrified them all except Niobe alone: she was bold in her misfortune. They were standing in black clothes before the funeral biers of their brothers – sisters with their hair untied; one of them, pulling out the arrows which clung to his flesh, pressed her face against her brother and grew faint as she died; a second tried to console her wretched mother and suddenly fell silent and was bent double with a hidden wound. Another one, fleeing in vain, sank down too, another died upon her sister; another one hid, you would have seen another trembling. When six had been given up to death and had suffered different wounds, the last remained: her mother, protecting her with her whole body, with all her clothers too, shouted, 'Leave just one, the youngest! Out of many, it is the youngest I ask for, just one.' While she asked, the one for whom she asked died: bereft of children she sank down amongst her lifeless sons, daughters and husband and grew rigid with her woes. The breeze moved not a hair, in her face her colouring was bloodless, her eyes stood motionless in her grieving cheeks, there was nothing living in her appearance.

Ovid, *Metamorphoses* 6.286-305

21. Love at first sight

As soon as Abas' descendant saw her, her arms tied to the hard rocks, if not for the fact that a light breeze had moved her hair and her eyes were were wet with warm tears, he would have thought her a work of marble; unaware he caught fire and was dumbfounded, and seized by the image of beauty which he saw, almost forgot to beat his wings in the air. When he alighted, he said, 'O you who do not deserve these chains, but those with which desirous lovers are joined to each other, reveal to one who asks it the name of your country and your own, and why you wear shackles.' At first she was silent, nor did she, a maiden, dare to address a man, and she would have hidden her bashful face with her hands, if she had not been bound fast; her eyes – this much she could do – she filled with the tears which had welled up. As he urged her repeatedly, she explained to him, so that she might not seem to be refusing to reveal some faults of her own, the name of her country and her own, and how great her mother's belief had been in her beauty, and before she had told him every-thing, a wave crashed, and advancing towards them a monster loomed up over the boundless sea, breasting the broad ocean.

Ovid, *Metamorphose*s 4.672-690

22. A flood

And now the sea and the land had no distinction: all was sea, and a sea that had no shores. One man occupies a hill-top, whilst another sits in a curved boat and plies oars there where recently he ploughed; one sails above corn-fields or the rooftops of a submerged house, another catches a fish at the top of an elm-tree. An anchor, if it so chances, is fixed in a green meadow, or curved keels brush over vineyards lying beneath; and where just recently graceful goats grazed upon grass, there shapeless seals now place their bodies. The Nereids marvel at groves, cities and houses beneath the water, and dolphins occupy the woods, bumping into lofty branches and shaking oak trees as they knock against them. The wolf swims among the sheep, and the waves bear along tawny lions, and tigers too; neither his lightning strength avails the boar, nor his swift legs the stag swept away. And after seeking long the land where he might rest, the wandering bird falls with weary wings down into the sea. The measureless licence of the sea had overwhelmed the hills, and strange waves beat upon the mountain-peaks.

Ovid, *Metamorphoses* 1.291-310

23. Love lost for the second time

And now as he retraced his steps he had avoided all dangers, and the restored Eurydice was coming to the upper air, following behind (for Proserpina had made this condition), when a sudden madness seized the unwary lover, to be forgiven indeed, if only Hell knew how to forgive. He stopped, and already on the very brink of daylight, forgetful –alas! – and defeated in his purpose, looked back at his own [dear] Eurydice. In that moment all his toil was undone and the pact of the ruthless tyrant broken, and three times a crash was heard over the pools of Avernus. 'What frenzy,' she said, 'what frenzy so great, Orpheus, has destroyed both you and unhappy me? Lo, again the cruel fates call me back and sleep closes my swimming eyes. And now, farewell; I am borne away, wrapped in great darkness and stretching out to you, alas no longer yours, my strengthless hands.' She spoke, and suddenly fled away from his sight, just like smoke mingling into thin air, and no longer did she see him, vainly clutching at the shadows and wishing to say much. Nor did the ferryman of Orcus let him cross again the barrier of the marsh.

Virgil, *Georgics* 4.485-503

24. Sea-snakes

Through such traps and the deceitful Sinon's skill his story was believed, and they were overcome by tricks and false tears, men whom neither the son of Tydeus, nor Achilles of Larissa, nor ten years conquered, nor a thousand ships. At this point, something else greater and much more to be feared was presented to us poor wretches and disturbed our unwary hearts. Laocoon, Neptune's priest chosen by lot, was sacrificing a huge bull at the appointed altars. But look! Through the calm deep waters, from Tenedos two snakes with huge coils (I shudder as I tell it) towered over the sea and side by side made for the shore; their chests, held high among the waves, and their bloody crests rose above the waters; the rest of them passed through the sea behind and they twisted their huge backs in a coil. There was noise as the sea-water foamed, and already they were reaching the land; and, their blazing eyes suffused with blood and fire, they kept licking their hissing mouths with quivering tongues. We fled, pale at the sight. They, in steady procession, made for Laocoon; and first, each snake, having embraced the small bodies of his two sons, wound around them and ate up their wretched limbs with a bite.

Virgil, *Aeneid* 2.195-215

Translations of Further Unseens

1. Opposition to Caesar

When the senate has been dismissed in the evening, all who are of that order are summoned by Pompey. He praises the eager and heartens them for the future, while he criticises and stimulates the less energetic. Everywhere many from Pompey's old armies are called out in the hope of rewards and promotion, and many are summoned from the two legions which have been handed over by Caesar. The city and the comitium itself are filled with tribunes, centurions and reserves. All the friends of the consuls, all the supporters of Pompey and of those who nursed long-lasting enmity towards Caesar, are forced to attend the senate. By their vociferous gathering the weaker are terrified, the doubtful are strengthened, and the majority are denied the ability to make a free decision. Lucius Piso, the censor, promises to go to Caesar, likewise Lucius Roscius, the praetor, to inform him of these matters. They demand an interval of six days for carrying out this matter. Also opinions are expressed by some that ambassadors should be sent to Caesar to put before him the feelings of the senate.

All of these are resisted, and are opposed by the speeches of the consul, of Scipio and of Cato. Cato is goaded on by his old hatred towards Caesar and his distress over his defeat.

Caesar, *De Bello Civili* 1.3-4

2. Tall Poppies

Therefore, since he was gradually stirring up the leaders of the Gabini to renew hostilities, and was himself going out on raids and forays with the boldest of the young men, and since, as all his words and deeds were calculated to deceive, an ill-founded trust in him was growing, Sextus was at last appointed commander-in-chief of the war. When in the course of this, the people still unaware of what was going on, skirmishes took place between Rome and Gabii in which, as a rule, the Gabian cause had the upper hand, the highest and the lowest of the Gabini began to believe that it was by the gift of the gods that Sextus Tarquinius had been sent to them as a leader. Amongst the soldiers, indeed, by facing dangers along with them and by generously distributing booty, he was held in such affection that Tarquin the father was not more powerful at Rome than was the son at Gabii. Therefore, once he saw that enough strength had been gathered for any undertaking, he sent one of his men to his father in Rome, to ask what at all he wanted him to do, in that the gods had granted him sole power in all official matters at Gabii. No verbal reply was given to this messenger, I imagine because he seemed to be of dubious loyalty; rather the king, as if deep in thought, passed into the garden of his house, followed by his son's messenger. Walking up and down there in silence, he is said to have struck off with his staff the tallest poppy-heads. Tired by putting his question and waiting for a reply, the messenger returned to Gabii, regarding his mission a failure. He reported what he himself had said and what he had seen: whether from anger, hatred or his natural arrogance the king had uttered not a word. Once it was clear to Sextus what his father wanted, or what instruction he was giving with his silent riddles, he eliminated the leading men of the state without delay. Many were executed openly, some in secret.

Livy 1.54

3. Against Antony

It remains, citizens, that you persist in that view which you openly display. I shall act therefore as generals usually do when their battle line is already drawn up, so that, even though they see their men absolutely prepared for the fight, they may nevertheless encourage them. Your contest, citizens, is not with the sort of enemy with whom any terms of peace are possible. For it is not for your enslavement, as before, that he has become desirous, but rather, now, in anger, for your blood. No game seems to him more pleasant than bloodshed, than slaughter, than the butchery of citizens before his eyes. You are not dealing, Romans, with a wicked and villainous man, but with a foul and monstrous beast; since he has fallen into the pit, let him be overwhelmed. For, if he emerges from it, there is no punishment, however cruel, it will be possible to avoid. But he is held fast, pressed and harassed now by the forces which we already have, and soon by those which the new consuls will acquire in a few days time. Devote yourselves, Romans, to the cause as you are doing. Never has your agreement been greater in any cause, never have you been so strongly allied with the senate. And no wonder; for what is at stake is not on what terms we shall live, but rather whether we shall live, or perish with punishment and ignominy.

Cicero, Philippic 4.5.11

4. Drawings in the sand

Ulysses was not handsome, but was eloquent, yet he tormented goddesses of the sea with love. Ah, how often Calypso grieved that he was hurrying on his way, and said that the waters were not fit for rowing! Again and again she asked to hear the fate of Troy: often would he tell the same tale in a different way. They had stopped on the shore: there too lovely Calypso demands the gory fate of the Odrysian chief. He, with a light staff (for he chanced to be holding a staff), draws in the thick sand the task she requests. 'This,' he says, 'is Troy (he made walls on the shore); let this be the Simois; and imagine that this is my camp. There were the tents of Sithonian Rhesus; and this is the way I rode back by night when I'd captured the horses.' And he was drawing more, when a sudden wave removed Pergama and Rhesus' camp along with its leader. Then the goddess said, 'Those waters which you believe you can trust on your journey, do you see what mighty names they have wiped out!'

Ovid, *Ars Amatoria* 2.122-39

5. Joyous love

Here she will be: here she has sworn to remain. My enemies may burst! We have won: she could not stand out against the constant prayers. Greedy envy may lay aside its false delight: our Cynthia has stopped travelling unfamiliar routes. To her I am dear, and thanks to me Rome is said to be the dearest place in the world, and she says that no kingdom would please her without me. She has chosen to sleep with me even on a narrow bed, and to be mine in any way at all, rather than to have the ancient kingdom that was Hippodamia's dowry and the wealth that Elis, fit for horses, long ago acquired. Although he was giving much and promising more, she still did not greedily flee from my embrace. Her I managed to sway, not with gold, not with Indian pearls, but with a gift of charming song. The Muses do exist then; and Apollo is not slow to aid a lover; it is these I rely on in my love: exquisite Cynthia is mine. Now I may touch the stars above with my palms: come day, or come night, she is mine; and a rival will not steal away my love, which is sure. That boast will be familiar to my old age.

Propertius 1.8B.27-46
Trans S.J. Heyworth

6. Foul murder

Unhappy Priam had once secretly entrusted this Polydorus to the Thracian king to bring him up together with a great weight of gold, when he was already losing confidence in the arms of Dardania and saw that the city was encircled in a siege. But he, when the power of the Trojans was broken and Fortune withdrew, followed Agamemnon's cause and his victorious arms and abused all that was right: he slaughtered Polydorus and gained his gold by violence. To what do you not drive the hearts of men, you cursed hunger for gold! After fear had left my bones, I told the portents of the gods to the chosen leaders of the people, my father first, and I asked them what they thought. All held the same opinion, to depart from the accursed land, to leave the place where hospitality had been violated, and to give our fleet the south winds. Therefore we performed new funeral rites for Polydorus, and earth was heaped high on the mound; altars were built to the spirits of the dead, sad with dark blue ribbons and black cypress, and around them stood the women of Troy with the hair untied as was the custom; we brought cups foaming with warm milk and broad shallow bowls of sacred blood, and we laid the spirit to rest in a tomb and called upon it in a loud voice in the final summons.

Virgil, *Aeneid* 3.49-68

Versions of Prose Compositions

Latin Composition 1

hoc nuntio accepto, Caesar, ubi omnes copias convocavit, ad tribunal progressus orationem huiusmodi habuit: 'consilia hostium, milites, e speculatoribus iam cognovimus. pauci, quod pugnare timent, ad oppida vicosque proximos pedem rettulerunt; plerique tamen rati se facile nos multis cladibus iam fractos vincere posse, se in has silvas abdiderunt, atque in animo habent cras prodire ut prima luce proelium nobiscum committant. quae cum ita sint, vos nunc moneo ut ad tabernacula redeatis cenamque paretis; mane enim summa vi pugnandum erit ad patriam servandam.' quibus verbis confirmati, milites magna voce clamare coeperunt; mox alii cibum parabant, alii arma congerebant. pauci tamen adeo terrebantur ut paulisper inter se collocuti fugae se mandare constituerint. media igitur nocte furtim e castris discesserunt domosque petiverunt.

Latin Composition 2

Scipio Nasica, senator praeclarissimus, olim ad Ennium poetam, amicum suum, venit, ut eum de re gravissima consuleret. cum tamen ad villam eius advenisset amicumque ab ostio quaesivisset, ancilla dominum intus esse negavit. Scipio autem, suspicatus eam mentiri iussuque domini hoc respondisse, iratus se convertit nec plura locutus celeriter discessit. paucis post diebus Ennius, quod verebatur ne tali fraude amicum amisisset, illum visere constituit. ubi tamen ianuam pulsavit, Scipio ipse magna voce clamavit se non esse domi, amicoque severe imperavit ut abiret. quo audito Ennius, 'noli, mi amice,' inquit, 'me decipere conari. nonne vocem tuam agnosco?' sed Scipio respondit eum hominem esse impudentem. 'si enim,' inquit, 'ego ancillae tuae credidi, nonne tu mihi ipsi credere debes?'

Latin Composition 3

Horatius autem superatis interfectisque tribus Curiatiis, exercitum victorem Romam iam reducebat. hac victoria patria servata erat, et omnes cives aderant qui eum spolia belli in urbem ferentem cum gaudio salutarent. ingredienti tamen illi per Portam Capenam obviam iit soror virgo, quae uni ex illis quos frater interfecerat clam desponsa erat. cognito tum super umeros eius paludamento quod ipsa fecerat, dolore superata sponsum suum nomine appellavit. quo audito, Horatius adeo irascebatur ut gladio stricto puellam ilico confoderit. id facinus et patribus et plebi atrox visum est, iuvenisque comprehensus in iudicium adductus est. cum tamen pater eius adfirmavisset filiam iure poenas perfidiae suae dedisse, civesque ne se omnibus liberis orbum facerent oravisset, iudices, lacrimis senis permoti, laudata virtute Horatium absolverunt.

Latin Composition 4

Tarquinius Superbus, vir nec iustus nec populo carus, ultimus rex erat Romanorum. olim, cum regnaret, serpens e columna lignea elapsus tanto pavore perculit pectora omnium qui aderant, ut rex constituerit duos e filiis Delphos mittere qui deum rogarent quid faciendum esset. praeterea, quod hoc iter illo tempore maxime periculosum erat, comitem dedit illis filium sororis, L. Iunium Brutum, iuvenem ingeniosum, sed qui semper simulabat se stultum esse, ne ab avunculo interficeretur.

responso autem Apollinis audito, filii regis deum rogaverunt uter Romae rex futurus esset. hic statim eis respondit eum qui primus osculum matri dedisset imperium summum ibi habiturum esse. tum Titus Arrunsque Brutum hoc cuiquam patefacere vetuerunt; ille tamen, quia intellegebat quid deus re vera significaret, prolapsus terram osculatus est, matrem communem omnium mortalium.

Latin Composition 5

cum Marius in vincula Minturnis coniectus esset, servus quidam publicus, Germanus natu, missus est ad eum interficiendum. Marius autem, ubi illum stricto gladio appropinquare vidit, 'num tu,' inquit, 'servus imperatorem Gaium Marium interficere audebis?' quibus verbis auditis, servus abiecto gladio e carcere cucurrit, exclamans se tantum virum, qui tot vicisset hostes populi Romani, interficere timere. deinde Minturnenses, quippe qui crederent a deis iniectum esse servo terrorem, Mario e carcere emisso, traditis vestimentis viaticoque, navem paraverunt qua in Africam veheretur. ubi cum apud Carthaginienses moraretur, ad eum venit lictor Sextii praetoris, qui Africam tunc obtinebat, imperavitque ut praetoris iussu sine mora e provincia discederet. diu Marius silebat, quasi nihil audivisset; sed lictori tandem roganti num quid referri vellet, 'nuntia', inquit, 'te Gaium Marium vidisse Carthaginis inter ruinas sedentem.'

Latin Composition 6

ubi Hostius cecidit, statim copiae Romanae loco cedere coeperunt, Romulus ipse turba militum fugientium ad veterem portam Palatii actus est. ibi, arma ad caelum tollens, magna voce 'Iuppiter,' inquit, 'tuis iussus avibus hic in Palatio prima urbis fundamenta posui; arcem captam iam habent Sabini; inde armati tam celeriter trans vallem progrediuntur ut brevi adfuturi sint; at tu, pater deum hominumque, hostes hinc discedere coge; solitam Romanis redde virtutem fugamque siste; equidem promitto me, si nobis subveneris, templum tibi hic aedificaturum quod monumentum sit posteris auxilio tuo servatam esse urbem.' haec precatus, rex statim credere visus est deum se audivisse. 'hic, Romani,' inquit, 'Iuppiter optimus maximus vos consistere proeliumque renovare iubet.' quibus verbis auditis, Romani, quasi divina voce iussi, duci paruerunt; ac Romulus cum manu iuvenum ferocissimorum impetum fecit hostesque reppulit.

Latin Composition 7

hac oratione ab Diviciaco habita, omnes qui aderant multis lacrimis auxilium a Caesare petere coeperunt. ille tamen animadvertit solos ex omnibus Sequanos nihil earum rerum facere quas ceteri facerent, sed tristes capite demisso terram intueri. cuius rei quae causa esset miratus, illos rogavit cur tam miseri viderentur. Sequani autem nihil responderunt, sed tristes tacitique ut antea permanebant. si iterum illos hoc rogavisset Caesar, responsum fortasse dedissent; sed priusquam hoc accideret, Diviciacus ipse ad hunc modum respondit: Sequanos omnibus ceteris miseriores esse; illos enim solos neque queri neque auxilium implorare audere, sed Ariovisti etiam absentis crudelitatem, velut si coram adesset, semper horrere. his rebus cognitis, Caesar Gallorum animos verbis benignis confirmavit, pollicitusque est sibi eam rem curae futuram esse.

Latin Composition 8

Romanis autem cum Volscis bellum iam gerentibus, Sextus Tarquinius, filius regis, ad vicinum oppidum Volscorum, Gabios nomine, se contulit, simulans se hostem esse populi Romani. ibi totiens Gabinos et dictis et factis adiuvit ut brevi credere inciperent deos sibi hunc iuvenem ducem belli misisse. at ille, simul ac satis auctoritatis apud eos adeptus est, quendam ex suis Romam misit qui cognosceret quid pater se facere vellet. cum tamen nuntius eo advenisset et in regiam adductus esset, rex nihil voce respondit, sed in hortum statim exiit. ibi, tacitus inter flores ambulans, summa papaverum capita gladio desecuit, nuntioque ut ad filium rediret imperavit. qui sine mora Gabios regressus filio rettulit quid accidisset: seu ira seu superbia regem nullum dedisse responsum. Sextus tamen facile intellegere poterat quid pater significaret, omnesque Gabinorum principes comprehensos supplicio affecit.

Latin Composition 9

Curio, ubi perterritis omnibus intellexit quantus esset hostium exercitus, statim copiis suis imperavit ut proximos peterent colles. hos quoque occupaverant equites ab imperatore hostium praemissi. tum vero ad summam desperationem nostri pervenerunt, multique fugere conantes ab hostibus occisi sunt. si Curio ipse se fugae mandare voluisset, facile in salutem effugere potuit. affirmavit tamen numquam se, amisso exercitu quem a Caesare accepisset, in eius conspectum rediturum esse; atque ita fortiter proelians interfectus est. pauci equites, qui ad equos reficiendos priore die in oppido remanserant, tandem incolumes in castra regressi sunt; sed ceteri, et omnes pedites, ad unum trucidati sunt.

Latin Composition 10

interea Graeci, ne cibo omnino carerent, iumenta caedere coacti sunt; deinde, collectis sagittis, scutis, aliisque proelii reliquiis quas haud procul a castris invenerunt, igne facto cibum coquere coeperunt. circa fere meridiem advenerunt nuntii quidam a rege Persarum, comitante Phalino Zacynthio qui ob peritiam rei militaris summa erat apud Tissaphernem auctoritate. his imperatum erat ut Graecos iuberent se armis statim depositis regis arbitrio submittere. vix haec nuntiaverant mandata cum Clearchus, dux Graecorum, ad victimas quasdam inspiciendas avocatus est. tantum igitur ideo moratus ut victores negaret arma tradere solere, collegis imperavit ut tale referrent responsum quale eis maxime idoneum videretur et statim discessit.

Latin Composition 11

at coniurati, simul ac limen intraverunt, foribus obseratis, Philippum in lecto iacentem invaserunt, catenis vinxerunt. statim in regia ortus est tumultus, tantus vero ut etiam foris exaudiri posset. atque hic facile intellegi potest quam invisa sit infinita potestas, quam misera vita eorum qui metui malint quam amari; cum enim coniurati, qui forte inermes erant, telum flagitarent quo regem conficerent, fortasse stipatores eius, si benevoli fuissent, foribus effractis eum servare conati essent. nemo tamen illi succurrebat; et interea Thrax quidam, Seuthes nomine, parvum per fenestram intromisit pugionem, quo sine mora Philippus interfectus est.

Latin Composition 12

atqui nonnulli sunt in hoc ordine, patres conscripti, qui aut non videant aut videre nolint quid reipublicae immineat, qui spem Catilinae mollibus sententiis aluerunt coniurationemque eius nascentem non credendo corroboraverunt. quorum auctoritate multi cives, non solum improbi sed etiam ignari, si de Catilina poenas dignas nuper sumpsissem, me regie et crudeliter fecisse certe dixissent. nunc vero pro certo habeo, si iste se copiis Manlianis paucis diebus iunxerit, neminem tam stultum fore ut non videat coniurationem esse factam, neminem tam improbum ut non fateatur. si enim Catilinam unum supplicio adfecerimus, patres, bene scio hanc patriae nostrae pestem paulisper reprimi, non in perpetuum comprimi posse; quodsi iste se in exsilium eiecerit secumque suos omnes eduxerit, exstinguetur atque delebitur non modo haec reipublicae pestilentia, verum etiam stirps ac semen malorum omnium.

4. Translations of Passages for Exploration

1. Virgil, *Aeneid* 1.272-96

Here there shall be rule by kings for a full span of three hundred years under Hector's race, until Ilia, a royal princess, pregnant by Mars, shall give birth to two sons. Then Romulus, rejoicing in the tawny covering of the she-wolf nursing him, will take over the rule of the Roman race and will build the walls of Mars and will call his people Romans after his own name. For them I set no bounds in space or time: I have given them rule without end. And what is more, savage Juno, who now troubles the sea, the earth and the sky with fear, will change her thoughts for the better and will join with me in cherishing the Romans, lords of the world, a people wearing the toga. This is what has been decided. There shall come a time as the years roll by when the house of Assaracus will reduce Phthia and famous Mycenae to slavery and rule over the conquered Argives. There shall be born a Trojan of noble lineage, Caesar, who shall bound his empire by Ocean, his glory by the stars, Julius, a name passed down from great Iulus. In time to come, have no fear, you will receive him in heaven, laden with spoils from the East. He also will be invoked in prayers. Then wars will cease and the savage centuries will soften; grey-haired Faith, and Vesta, and Quirinus with his brother Remus will be law-givers; the gates of War, terrible in their close-wrought frame of iron, shall be shut; and impious Frenzy will sit inside on a pile of savage arms, his hands tied behind his back with a hundred knots of bronze, bellowing hideously from his bloody mouth.

2a. Catullus 3

Mourn, o Venuses and Cupids, and all you more charming types! The sparrow of my girl is dead, the sparrow, the darling of my girl, which she loved more than her eyes. For it was as sweet as honey and knew its mistress as well as a girl knows her mother, and it didn't move from her lap, but hopping around now this way, now that, it used to chirp continually only to its mistress. Now it is going on that shadowy journey from which they say nobody returns. But may it go badly with you, you bad shadows of Orcus, who devour all beautiful things: you have robbed me of such a beautiful sparrow! It's your doing that the little eyes of my girl are swollen and red with weeping.

2b. Catullus 7

You ask how many of your kisses, Lesbia, are enough and more than enough for me. As great a number as the Libyan sands which lie in silphium-bearing Cyrene between the oracle of sweltering Jupiter and the sacred tomb of old

Battus: or as many as the stars that, when the night is silent, see the stolen loves of men: that is the number of kisses that are enough and more than enough for you to kiss mad Catullus, a number which the curious could not count up nor evil tongue bewitch.

3. Tacitus, *Annals* 14.1-2 3

In the consulship of Gaius Vipstanus and Gaius Fonteius [59 AD], Nero no longer postponed a crime which he had long meditated: his boldness had grown stronger because of the length of his reign, and his love for Poppaea grew more passionate with each day. She saw no hope of marriage for herself and divorce for Octavia while Agrippina remained unharmed, and from time to time would criticise the emperor by mocking him. She said that he was acting as if he weren't a grown-up: he was submitting to other people's orders and was not only wihout his supreme authority but without his freedom. Otherwise why was marriage with her being postponed? No doubt her beauty and her victorious ancestors were displeasing to him, or the fact that she could bear children or was sincere in her love? Was the fear that, if she actually became his wife, she would expose the injuries done to the senate and the people's anger against the pride and greed of his mother. But if Agrippina could put up with no daughter-in-law except one who hated her son, could she (Poppaea) please be returned to Otho as his wife: she would go anywhere on earth where she could hear of the emperor's humiliations rather than witness them and be caught up in his dangers. Nobody stopped these words and others like them which got through to Nero because of her tears and the arts of an adulteress: everybody wanted the mother's power to be broken and no-one believed that her son's hatred would go as far as her murder.

Cluvius records that in her passion to hold on to power she went so far that in the middle of the day, at the time when Nero's temperature was raised by wine and food, she several times offered herself to her drunken son, all dressed up and ready for incest; and now, when those closest to them observed their sexy kisses and their caresses that indicated that something shocking was about to happen, Seneca sought help against a woman's ensnarements from a woman, and the freedwoman Acte was sent to Nero; she, in her anxiety at one and the same time about her danger and Nero's notoriety, was to inform him that the rumour was spreading that he was committing incest and his mother was boasting of the fact, and that the soldiers would not tolerate rule by a sacrilegious emperor.

4. Livy 23.2

Then Hannibal veered to Capua, (a city) luxuriating in its long prosperity and the generosity of fortune, but, amid the general corruption, above all in the license of the common people who enjoyed freedom without limits. Pacuvius Calavius had made the senate answerable to him and to the people. He was a noble who was at the same time a supporter of the people, but he had gained his influence by bad methods. It so happened that in the year of the defeat at Lake Trasimene he held their chief magistracy, and he thought that the people, who had now for a long time been hostile to the senate, would take the opportunity of a revolution and dare to commit a great crime, i.e. that if Hannibal came into their region with his victorious army, they would slaughter the senate and hand over Capua to the Carthaginians. He was a bad man but not totally depraved since he preferred to be dominant in an intact state rather than one which had been destroyed, but believed that no state could be intact if it was deprived of its deliberative body, and so he embarked on a scheme to save the senate and to make it subservient to himself and the people. He summoned the senate and said at the start that he would not in any way approve of a plan to defect from the Roman people unless it was necessary (to do so), seeing that he had children by a daughter of Appius Claudius and had given a daughter in marriage to Marcus Livius at Rome; but (he said) there was the threat of something much greater and more to be feared; for the people were not looking to remove the senate from the state by revolting, but wanted by the slaughter of the senate to hand over the republic to Hannibal and the Carthaginians in a helpless condition; he could free them from that danger if they left it to him and, forgetting about their political struggles, put their trust in him. When all of them were overcome by fear and left it to him, he said, 'I shall shut you in the senate house and, as if I myself too were a party to the crime, by approving plans which it would be pointless to oppose, I shall find a way to win you safety. Receive the pledge for this that you yourselves ask for.' After he had given the pledge, he went out, ordered the senate house to be shut, and left a guard in the entrance so that nobody could enter the senate house or leave it without orders from him.

5. Virgil, *Aeneid* 4.66-89

All the time the flame is eating the soft marrow of her bones and the wound lives silently under her breast. The unhappy Dido is on fire and wanders all over the city in her frenzy like a deer hit by an arrow which a shepherd hunting in the woods of Crete has shot from afar, hitting her off her guard and leaving the winged steel in her flesh, unaware what he has done. In her flight she wanders through the wooded defiles of mount Dicte; the deadly arrow is sticking in her side. Now she leads Aeneas with her through the middle of the city and shows him the wealth of Sidon and the city that lies ready for him. She begins to speak and stops in mid-sentence. Now, as day is ending, she calls for that same banquet again, and in her madness demands to hear the tale of

Troy's sufferings once more and once more hangs from his lips as he tells it. Afterwards when they have parted and the dim moon subdues her light in its turn, and the setting stars are urging sleep, she grieves alone in her empty house and she throws herself on the couch he has left. He is not there and they are apart, but she hears him and she sees him. Or, captivated by his resemblance to his father, she holds back Ascanius on her lap in the hope that she may comfort a love she cannot speak of. The towers she has begun to build do not rise, the young men do not exercise in arms or build harbours or fortifications for safety in war. Everything has stopped, all the building, the huge threatening walls and the crane towering to the sky – all at a standstill.

6. Propertius 3.10

I was wondering why the Camenae had visited (me) of a morning, standing before my bed as the sun grew red. They sent a sign to celebrate my girl's birthday and thrice they propitiously clapped their hands. May this day pass without a cloud, the winds be still in the air, and the wave cease from threatening and be stilled on the dry shore. May I see no one grieving today, and let the very rock of Niobe suppress its tears; let the mouths of the halcyons lay aside their complaints and rest, and Itys' mother not moan over her dead son. [10] And you, my dear one, born under happy omens, rise and pray to the deities who demand what is due to them. First shake the sleep from yourself with pure water, and arrange your shining hair with finger pressed against thumb. Then put on the dress in which you first captured the eyes of Propertius, and do not leave your head free of flowers, and seek that your beauty (where your strength lies) be everlasting, and that your reign over me be established for ever. Then when you have consecrated the garlanded altars with incense, and a favourable flame has shone throughout the house, [20] let there be thought given to the table, and night run away amid our drinking, and a jar of perfume anoint our nostrils with saffron. (Trans. S.J. Heyworth.)

7. Tacitus, *Annals* 15.44

Soon after, they sought ways of appeasing the gods and the Sibylline books were consulted. As a result they addressed prayers to Vulcan, Ceres and Proserpina, and Juno was propitiated by the married women, first on the Capitol and then at the closest stretch of sea, from which water was taken to sprinkle the temple and the image of the goddess; and women whose husbands were living celebrated festivals for goddesses and vigils.

But neither human resources nor the emperor's largess nor appeasement of the gods banished the sinister suspicion that the fire had been started deliberately. Therefore, in order to eliminate the rumours, Nero invented scapegoats and subjected them to the most refined punishments: these were the people whom the crowd referred to as Christians and they were hated because of their crimes. The originator of the name (of Christian) was Christ who had been executed (suffered punishment) in the reign of Tiberius by the governor Pontius Pilate. The deadly superstition had been checked for a time, but was breaking out again, not just in Judaea where this evil began but even in the city, where everything horrible and shameful flows in from everywhere and flourishes. And so first those who confessed were arrested, and then through information given by them a vast number were convicted not so much for the charge of incendiarism as because of their hatred of the human race. And mockery was inflicted on them too as they died, with the result that, dressed in the hides of wild beasts, they perished torn to pieces by dogs or fixed to crosses or to be set on fire and, every time the daylight failed, they were burned to supply light at night. Nero had provided his gardens for the spectacle and put on an entertainment in the circus, at which he mingled with the people dressed as a charioteer or standing in a chariot. As a result, although it was aimed at guilty people who deserved the most extraordinary exemplary punishment, pity was roused on the grounds that they were being killed not for the public interest but because of one man's savagery.

8. Sallust, *Bellum Catilinae* 24-5

Therefore, after the elections had been held, Marcus Tullius (Cicero) and Gaius Antonius were declared consuls. The event had at first shaken the associates in the conspiracy. However, the frenzy of Catiline was not diminished, but he stirred things up more from day to day: he got ready resources for fighting in suitable locations over Italy, and carried money he had borrowed on his credit or that of his friends to Faesulae to a certain Manlius, who later was the first man to start the war. At that time he (Catiline) is said to have called to himself very many citizens of all sorts and conditions, and several women too who had at first sustained their huge expenditure by prostituting their bodies but later, when advancing years had set a limit on their ability to raise money but not on their luxurious lifestyle, had run up vast debts. Through these women Catiline believed that he could rouse the slaves of the city, set fire to the city, and either join their husbands to his cause or kill them.

But among them was Sempronia, a woman who had often committed many crimes of masculine audacity. This woman was pretty well blessed by fortune in her family and beauty, and in addition in her husband and children; she was educated in Greek and Latin literature, played the cithara, and danced with greater elegance that is necessary for a respectable woman. She pursued many other paths to excess (lit. means to indulgence) but everything always proved more dear to her than honour and chastity; you could not easily have told whether she was more careless (lit. less sparing) of her money or her reputation. But often before this time she had betrayed trust in her and forsworn a trust (i.e. she had kept money etc. entrusted to her). She had been an accomplice in murder. She had swerved headlong into luxury and poverty. But her nature was not despicable: she could compose poetry, speak wittily, and talk variously in a modest, appealing and shameless manner; in fact she possessed much wit and much charm.

9. Virgil, *Aeneid* 8.193-8

Here, receding to a vast depth, was the cave, never struck by the sun's rays, in which there lived a terrifying monster, the half-human Cacus. The ground was always wet with fresh blood and faces of men hung fixed to its proud portals, pale with horrible decay. Vulcan was the father of this monster. It was his black fires that he belched forth from his mouth as he moved along with his massive bulk. To us as we prayed, as to others, time at long last brought help with the arrival of the god. For the mighty avenger Hercules came this way, proudly driving his huge bulls, the spoils from the triple-bodied Geryon whom he had conquered and killed, and the bulls were at pasture in the valley and the river. But Cacus, his mind wild with frenzy, wished to ensure that he left no crime or trick undared or unattempted, and stole from their pasture four bulls of outstanding size and the same number of surpassingly fine heifers. And so that there should be no hoof-prints pointing in the right direction, the rustler dragged them into the cave by the tail to reverse the signs of where they had gone and hid them in the darkness of the rock. For anyone searching there were no traces pointing to the cave. Meanwhile, when the son of Amphitryon was now moving the well-fed herds from the pasturage and getting ready to go away, the cattle lowed as they went. The whole grove was filled with their complaints as they moved off bellowing from the hills. One of the cows returned the sound and mooed from deep in the vast cave, frustrating the hopes of the monster who held her prisoner. At this the black-galled anger of Hercules truly blazed up in his frenzy. He snatched up his arms and his heavy club of knotted oak in his hands and made for the heights of the lofty mountain at a run. Then for the first time our eyes beheld Cacus frightened and confused. At that moment he ran away more swiftly than the east wind and made for his cave. His fear gave his feet wings.

10. Cicero, *Pro Caelio* 31-80

However, first I shall enquire of the woman herself whether she prefers me to deal with her in a stern, solemn, antique manner or light-heartedly, playfully, in a smart modern way. If in that grim-styled way, I must call up from the dead one from among those big-bearded men (of old), not anyone with a neat little beard as they are now worn – which she delights in – but with that unkempt one which we see in ancient statues and busts, in order to rebuke the woman and speak instead of me, in case she may perhaps get angry with me. Arise then! – someone from this very family – and who better than the famous Caecus? – for he will be the least distressed: after all, he won't see her!

If he appears, I imagine that this is how he will treat her, this is what he will say: 'Woman, what business do you have with Caelius, with a man who is still a youth, with a stranger? Why have you been either so intimate with this man as to lend him gold or so hostile as to fear poison? Had you not seen that your father, had you not heard that your uncle, your grandfather, your great-grandfather, your great-great-grandfather, your great-great-great-grandfather were consuls? Finally, did you not know that you were married to Quintus Metellus, a most illustrious and courageous man and one most loving to his country, who, the moment he set foot out of doors, surpassed nearly all citizens in courage, glory and prestige? Since you had married from a most distinguished family into a most illustrious one, why was Caelius so linked with you? Was he a relative by blood, a connection by marriage, a close friend of your husband? None of these? What then was it but sheer wanton passion?

(The translation is indebted to R.G. Austin.)